BOMBING
FORTRESS EUROPE

by

Wallace B. Black
and
Jean F. Blashfield

CRESTWOOD HOUSE
New York

Maxwell Macmillan Canada
Toronto

Maxwell Macmillan International
New York Oxford Singapore Sydney

Library of Congress Cataloging-in-Publication Data

Black, Wallace B.
   Bombing fortress Europe / by Wallace B. Black and Jean F. Blashfield. —
1st ed.
      p.   cm. — (World War II 50th anniversary series)
   Includes index.
   Summary: Describes how British and American planes broke Hitler's
stranglehold on Europe and made bombing raids leading to the D-Day
invasion.
   ISBN 0-89686-562-2
   1. World War, 1939-1945 — Aerial operations, British — Juvenile literature.
2. World War, 1939-1945 — Aerial operations, American — Juvenile
literature. 3. Europe — History — Bombardment, 1939-1945 — Juvenile
literature. [1. World War, 1939-1945 — Aerial operations, British.
2. World War, 1939-1945 — Aerial operations, British. 2. World War,
1939-1945 — Aerial operations, American.] I. Blashfield, Jean F. II. Title.
III. Series: Black, Wallace B.
World War II 50th anniversary series.
D786.B53 1992
940.54'4941--dc20

                                                        91-31452
                                                           CIP
                                                            AC

Created and produced by B & B Publishing, Inc.

Picture Credits
Bettman Archives - page 20
Dave Conant, Map - page 24
Imperial War Museum - pages 9, 11, 15, 43
National Archives - pages 7, 21
United States Air Force - pages 3, 4, 9, 14, 18, 19, 22, 23, 27, 29, 30, 33, 35, 37, 39, 41, 44, 45

CRESTWOOD   Macmillan Publishing Company   Maxwell Macmillan Canada, Inc.
HOUSE   866 Third Avenue   1200 Eglinton Avenue East
                       New York, NY 10022   Suite 200
                                                         Don Mills, Ontario M3C 3N1

Macmillan Publishing Company is part of the Maxwell Communication Group of Companies.

Printed in the United States of America

First Edition

10 9 8 7 6 5 4 3 2 1

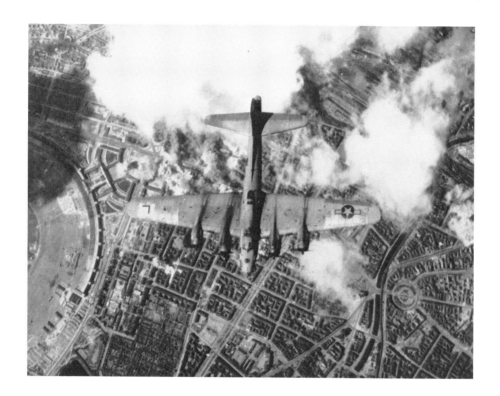

CONTENTS

Chapter 1

Hitler's Fortress Europe

In 1939 Europe was an armed camp. The nations of Europe feared a repetition of World War I, but they were forced to prepare for war because of events in Germany.

In the early 1930s Germany was still reeling from a severe economic depression and other problems brought on by the loss of World War I. The Germans elected Adolf Hitler as their new leader and dictator to help solve these problems. As soon as Hitler was able to achieve prosperity in Germany he began to rebuild the country's army, navy and air force.

By 1935 Hitler felt that Germany was strong enough to take over neighboring lands. Using the threat of force, Hitler was able to take back lands Germany had lost during World War I, including first the Saar and the Rhineland bordering on France and then Memel on Germany's northern border.

As these events were taking place, Germany's old enemies — France, Great Britain, Belgium and Holland — took notice and also began to rearm. They did not trust Hitler, but they did nothing to stop him. Germany annexed Austria and the Sudetenland in Czechoslovakia and in 1939 Germany expanded into the entire western half of that country.

War Returns to Europe

Finally the worst fears of the Allies became reality. On September 1, 1939, Germany invaded neighboring Poland from the west. At the same time Russia, Germany's ally,

A USAAF B-24 dives through heavy smoke to drop its bombs on the Ploesti oil refineries in Romania.

invaded Poland from the east. Although Poland's friends Great Britain and France immediately declared war on Germany, they could not stop the defeat of Poland.

Six months of major battles at sea but little action on land or in the air followed. Then full-scale war broke out again. In April 1940, Germany invaded and conquered Denmark and Norway. In May Holland, Belgium and France were overrun by the Germans. With Great Britain's help, these nations fought bravely against the Nazi *blitzkrieg* ("lightning-war") attacks.

However, the Allies were unprepared for Hitler's vicious and powerful asaults. By the end of June 1940, Hitler controlled all of central and most of western Europe. Italy joined with Germany and also declared war on the Allies. This left Great Britain to fight alone against the Nazi tyranny over Europe.

Air War the Only Answer

The English had suffered great losses of men and equipment during the battles to try and save Holland, Belgium and France. Expecting to be invaded by German forces at any time, they concentrated on defending their homeland. The Royal Navy, then the greatest navy on earth, fought bravely at sea. The navy defeated the German surface raiders and continued to fight against the growing threat of German U-boats (submarines).

Gradually, however, with aid coming from the United States and from British colonies, Great Britain built up its defenses. The Royal Air Force (RAF) fought off the German *Luftwaffe* (air force) successfully during the Battle of Britain. This was the air war that was fought over the British Isles during the last half of 1940. Between the RAF and the Royal Navy, the threatened German invasion was prevented.

By December of 1940, Britain was fighting a valiant defensive battle against the Germans. The country's only

An RAF Halifax four-engine bomber in flight. This heavy bomber, which saw action throughout the war, could carry 40,000 pounds of bombs.

offensive weapon against Germany and its conquered European lands was the RAF Bomber Command. Winston Churchill, the prime minister of Great Britain, told his people that since they could not fight the enemy on the ground, they must bomb them into submission from the air.

Target: Fortress Europe

Along with its allies Russia and Italy, Germany now controlled most of Europe. Great Britain had no means of launching land attacks against Europe. The continent had become a German fortress that was, for the time being, safe from invasion by an enemy.

Great Britain's only course of action was to bomb Hitler's "Fortress Europe." The RAF would eventually be joined by forces from the United States in 1942. Their combined efforts to bomb enemy war factories, military bases and airfields, cities and naval bases were continuous. There were four years of bombing before D-Day, the invasion of France in June 1944, and five years until the final surrender of Germany in 1945. The prolonged bombing of Germany — its cities and its military machine — led to final victory.

Chapter 2

THE BOMBERS WILL ALWAYS GET THROUGH

The idea that "bombers will always get through" had begun during World War I. The giant German Gotha bombers and Zeppelin airships bombed London successfully from 1915 to 1918. Allied bombers achieved similar success in bombing German cities in 1918.

Giulio Douhet, an Italian general, had developed the theory that a war could be won by bomber forces that destroyed the enemy's air force on the ground. One nation's bombers could destroy enemy aircraft, factories, airfields and air force before the enemy could destroy theirs. Bombers would be larger, fly farther and carry heavier bombloads and defensive armament.

War in Spain: A Testing Ground

During the Spanish Civil War in 1936, German and Russian bombers fighting in support of opposing forces went into action. Air raids were carried out against military and civilian targets by each side. Their success seemed to prove Douhet's theories.

In Great Britain the Bomber Command of the RAF was developed based on Douhet's ideas. Chief of the RAF Air Staff Sir Hugh Trenchard built up a bombing force and supporting fighter aircraft. In the United States, the U.S. Army Air Corps did the same.

A formation of Avro Anson light bombers in flight over the British countryside. Used for coastal patrol and as trainers, the Anson, like many RAF aircraft at the beginning of the war, was not suited for combat.

The RAF Goes to War

On paper the RAF was ready for war. Watching Hitler and his Nazi government rearm, the RAF began to build its force. By 1939 the RAF had an impressive fleet of twin-engine bombers. Supported by a small force of Hurricane and Spitfire fighter aircraft, the RAF had some 1,500 modern aircraft ready for war.

As part of Germany's attack on Poland, the Luftwaffe bombers attacked military and civilian targets throughout the country. Only a few German planes were lost as they destroyed the entire Polish air force on the ground. As an ally of Poland, Great Britain declared war on Germany on September 3, 1939.

The RAF Bomber Command went into action almost immediately. On September 4 they attacked German warships at Wilhelmshaven, Germany. Seven of the 29 RAF bombers were lost while they damaged only one German ship. That night a long-range mission was launched against German cities. But no bombs were dropped — only leaflets telling the German people that their leaders were evil and wrong in attacking Poland.

Chapter 3

RAF BOMBER COMMAND

The RAF was an independent military service, separate from the British army and navy. Opposed by the other services, it received little financial support. By 1939, however, a substantial air force had been built. Though quite impressive in theory, actually it was poorly prepared to fight a long-range war against a well-prepared enemy.

Basic Combat Flying Skills Lacking

In peacetime, RAF pilots had performed quite well. However, they had been poorly trained in radio, navigation, gunnery, bombing and bad-weather flying. This fact contributed to early failures and losses of aircraft as the RAF began the first daylight bombing attacks against German targets.

At first the RAF was prohibited from attacking targets in which German civilians might be harmed. As a result, they limited their targets to German warships at sea. They had little success. The RAF's so-called modern bombers were no match for German fighters.

Neither Great Britain nor France had any way to defend itself against German bombers. Both feared counterattacks if German civilian targets were bombed. So the RAF was not allowed to bomb German cities.

Daylight Bombing Fails

The RAF battle plan called for long-range daylight bombing attacks. These missions were to be carried out by

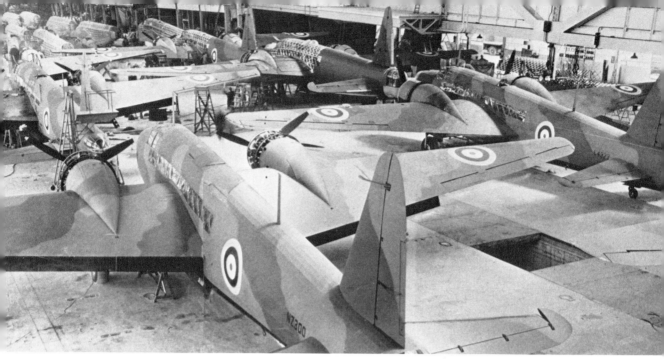
Wellington bombers under construction at a factory in England

heavy, two-engined bombers. Bombers such as the Wellington were relatively fast and were heavily armed.

On December 18, 1939, a force of 24 Wellingtons attacked German naval forces in the North Sea. Again the RAF was no match for the Luftwaffe. Me 109 and Me 110 Messerschmitt fighters destroyed 12 Wellingtons.

On May 10, 1940, the German *panzers* (tanks) finally struck again. Holland, Belgium and France were all attacked that day. The RAF and French air force could not defeat the Luftwaffe. All of their efforts to stop the German advance failed.

Holland, Belgium and France Surrender

Luftwaffe bombers, following Douhet's theories, constantly bombed and strafed Allied airfields. The Allies now only had RAF bases and aircraft in Great Britain. All Allied aircraft and airfields in Holland, Belgium and France had been destroyed or captured.

German panzers pushed the Allied forces to the beaches of France. The ineffective British Bomber Command was unable to stop the advance of the German *Wehrmacht* (army). RAF Fighter Command did provide air cover as the British successfully evacuated more than 300,000 troops from the beaches of Dunkirk.

For the time being Bomber Command was given a back-seat. Fighter Command fought the Battle of Britain, fending off attacking German bombers. Aircraft factories were kept busy building more fighters and pilots were being trained as quickly as possible.

Channel Invasion Threatened

Other developments slowed Bomber Command in its efforts to carry out the long-range raids on Germany. The few planes the British had were needed to attack the huge German invasion force that was gathering on the French coast.

During the month of September 1940, Bomber Command flew thousands of sorties (one mission by one aircraft) against the invasion ports. They accomplished their purpose, and German plans for invasion were cancelled. RAF Bomber Command was once again ready to start its night raids.

Mustering what planes it could, Bomber Command switched to night raids to start bombing targets in France and Germany. Without an Allied ground army on the continent, it would be up to the Bomber Command to destroy the enemy's ability to wage war. This began a five-year-long period of bombing Fortress Europe.

Long-Range Bombers of the RAF

RAF twin-engined Vickers Wellington and Armstrong Whitworth-Whitley bombers went into action. Luftwaffe bombing raids on civilian targets in Great Britain made the British people furious. They demanded raids against German cities. Bomber Command responded by ordering raids on industrial cities in France and Germany.

Such raids often failed to find and hit their targets, however, due to the inexperience of RAF crews. By December 1940, nighttime raids of 100 and more heavy bombers were attacking key military and industrial targets. As air crews became more experienced, results seemed to improve.

Newer four-engine bombers were already in production. The Stirling, Lancaster, Halifax and Manchester bombers carried heavy bombloads, were heavily armed and could fly long distances.

New Targets Assigned Once Again

German U-boats and pocket battleships were attacking British ships at sea. They were doing great damage to Allied shipping and slowing the delivery of supplies to Britain. Bomber Command was told to direct its efforts against German naval bases in Germany on the North Sea and their submarine bases in France.

Four major German battleships were destroyed or damaged and submarine pens on the French coast were heavily bombed. These strikes against German naval targets continued throughout 1941.

RAF Bomber Command's Main Mission

By 1942 it was finally determined that Bomber Command could operate most successfully at night using saturation bombing. Having seen the success of huge German raids on such English targets as London and Coventry, the RAF decided to use the same tactics. As a result, missions with hundreds of heavy bombers with tons of bombs began to pelt German industrial cities.

At this point, Bomber Command was assigned a new leader, Air Chief Marshal Arthur "Bomber" Harris. He ordered raids on key cities such as Renault in France and the German cities of Essen in the Ruhr Valley and Luebeck on the North Sea. Production of tanks at the Renault auto works was brought to a halt and the city of Luebeck was virtually destroyed.

At last larger and more powerful long-range four-engine bombers were being delivered. Raids of 100 and 200 planes were sent out almost nightly. Long-range saturation bombing of German military and civilian targets was becoming a reality.

Hitler was furious. For every German city bombed, he ordered the Luftwaffe to bomb another British city. Each bomber force was trying to destroy the other's ability to wage war and to destroy civilian morale.

The Thousand-Plane Raid

Bomber Command Air Chief Harris had decided that a force of 1,000 planes should carry out a giant raid on a key industrial city. To do this the Bomber Command had to beg, borrow or steal more than 1,000 planes from every branch of the RAF. A giant bomber fleet was finally ready for the massive attack against the major target chosen for the attack: Cologne, Germany.

The mission was a complete success. The attack started at a few minutes past midnight on May 30, 1940. Wave

General Dwight D. Eisenhower (second from left) *confers with British Air Chief Marshall Arthur Tedder* (left), *Field Marshall Bernard Montgomery* (right) *and an unidentified USAAF general.*

The city of Cologne, Germany, lay in ruins following the first 1,000-plane raid on Germany by RAF Bomber Command aircraft.

after wave of British bombers struck their target. Incendiary bombs lit up the darkened city to make a brilliant target for the groups that followed. More than 1,000 planes dropped over 1,500 tons of high explosives on the doomed city. Factories vital to the German war effort were destroyed. Hundreds of Germans died that night and over 40,000 were left homeless.

Although Bomber Command did some pinpoint raids on specific targets, its main mission was nighttime saturation bombing. Many missions were successful, but quite often poor navigation, bad weather and other problems caused bombs to miss their targets. During 1943 and 1944, RAF Bomber Command flew over 75,000 nighttime sorties and dropped over 200,000 tons of bombs on German targets. Although great damage was done to German targets, it was at a cost of over 2,600 British bombers shot down and the loss of some 25,000 brave crew members.

Chapter 4

THE EIGHTH AIR FORCE IS BORN

The clouds of war began to threaten young men in America as battles raged in Europe and bombs were dropped on Poland, England and Germany. Millions of men were called to active duty in the U.S. armed services and especially into the Army Air Corps, which was soon to be renamed the United States Army Air Force (USAAF).

Aviation cadets were being trained by the thousands. After the December 7, 1941 Japanese attack on Pearl Harbor in Hawaii, the training speeded up and tens of thousands more brave young men took to the air. The training of bomber crews was given top priority. An air force of 3,500 planes had been ordered to help the British in the continued bombing of Hitler's Fortress Europe.

General Eaker Takes Command

Lieutenant General Henry H. "Hap" Arnold, chief of the Army Air Corps, chose Brigadier General Ira C. Eaker to prepare the way for this huge new air force. Designated the Eighth Air Force, it would be made up of bomber and fighter aircraft necessary to carry the war from Great Britain across the English Channel to Germany.

Eaker acquired the land and arranged for the construction of all of the airfields, buildings and other facilities that would be needed. These airfields were located in the easternmost portion of England, called East Anglia.

General Ira Eaker (right), commander of the Eighth Air Force Bomber Command, discussing mission plans with one of his generals

The Eighth Air Force Takes Shape

General Eaker and the first units of the Eighth Air Force arrived in England on February 20, 1942. Bad weather and labor shortages made the construction of airfields slow and difficult. But in July, when the first Eighth Air Force bombers arrived, the fields were ready.

The Boeing B-17, named the Flying Fortress, and the Consolidated Vultee B-24 Liberator were the two long-range bombers assigned to the Eighth Air Force. With a range of 1,100 miles with full fuel and bombloads, they were heavily armored and had power turrets with .50 caliber machine guns. They were equipped with the highly accurate, top-secret Norden bombsight.

The first Eighth Air Force air crews arrived in England in May 1942 but without aircraft. Their aircraft were being delivered by ship. These first air crews were part of the 15th Bombardment Squadron. They were trained to fly twin-engine Douglas A-20 Havocs.

In July 1942, aircraft, men and equipment began to arrive in a steady stream. The Eighth Air Force grew rapidly. By 1944 this great air force would grow to over 200,000 men and 4,000 aircraft.

The First Mission

General Eaker was anxious to launch a mission against the Germans. He didn't want to wait for a B-17 group that was due to arrive, so he borrowed some A-20s from the RAF. The pilots of the 15th Bombardment Squadron would fly these aircraft. On July 4, 1942, American pilots flew the first USAAF mission from British soil against Luftwaffe airfields in Holland. Three A-20s were shot down but several enemy airfields were hit. American pilots had joined the war against the Nazis at last.

In July, B-17s began to arrive in a slow but steady stream. Flying the 2,100 miles over water from Gander Air Base in Newfoundland, Canada, to Prestwick, Scotland, was a difficult and dangerous mission. It was especially difficult for young and inexperienced pilots. The weather over the North Atlantic was often bad, and there were limited navigational aids.

U.S. Air Crews Need More Training

The 97th Bombardment Group had finally arrived with almost a full complement of aircraft and crews. Several

A-20 light bombers on a mission over France

A grim-faced bombardier beside a .50 caliber machine gun in the nose of a B-17 bomber

aircraft had been lost to bad weather in Greenland. The crews, however, were not yet ready for combat. General Eaker ordered additional training. Experienced British air crews helped train the American crews.

Harris and other British airmen tried to convince the Americans that their plans to carry out daylight bombing raids were suicidal. They wanted the American forces to join with the RAF Bomber Command in nighttime raids. But Eaker and his new boss, Lieutenant General Carl Spaatz, stood fast.

The USAAF heavy bombers were intended to fly daylight missions in large, close formations of B-17s and B-24s. Their heavy firepower and armor would enable them to fight off enemy fighters. Daylight precision bombing was their goal. It was claimed that with the Norden bombsight an American bomber could hit a pickle barrel from an altitude of 20,000 feet.

Eighth Air Force's First B-17 Mission

Finally, on August 17, 1942, 12 B-17 bombers of the 97th Bombardment Group roared down the runway at their base in eastern England. Eighth Bomber Command Mission Number One had taken off. Under the command of Colonel

Frank A. Armstrong, this first USAAF mission was escorted by four squadrons of RAF Spitfire fighters. Their target was the railroad yards at Rouen, France, 200 miles to the east.

German fighters intercepted the 97th as they approached the target. Wary of the heavy firepower of the B-17s and frightened off by the Spitfire fighters, the Luftwaffe fighters did not attack. The 97th dropped bombs directly on their target and all planes returned safely. It was a great day for the USAAF.

During the next six weeks Eaker's Eighth Bomber Command flew another dozen short missions against Luftwaffe bases in Holland, Belgium and France. With Spitfire and U.S. Lockheed P-38 Lightning fighters providing escort, the German fighters still did not attack. However, on September 6, new Focke-Wulfe FW 190 fighters attacked and shot down two U.S. bombers.

The Luftwaffe Comes to Life

On October 8 the USAAF launched its most ambitious mission. A force of 108 B-17s and B-24s took off for Lille, France. The mission had bad luck from the start. The weather was bad, and about 30 aircraft had mechanical

The smiling crew of B-17 Flying Fortress Nora's Wiles *all hold up six fingers indicating the number of German fighters they have shot down.*

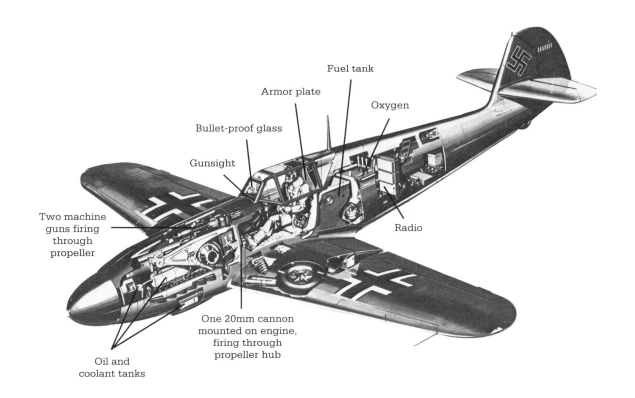

Fuel tank

Armor plate

Oxygen

Bullet-proof glass

Gunsight

Two machine
guns firing
through
propeller

Radio

One 20mm cannon
mounted on engine,
firing through
propeller hub

Oil and
coolant tanks

A cutaway drawing of the Luftwaffe Me 109. This great fighter was first used during the Spanish Civil War. From 1939 to the end of World War II the Me 109 was one of Germany's great defensive weapons.

problems and turned back. As the remaining aircraft of the bomber group approached their target, they were attacked by a force of over 60 Focke-Wulfe defending fighters — "bandits," as the U.S. air crews called them.

The bomber formation broke up and only a few bombs even came near their intended targets. Three B-17s and one B-24 were shot down and many of the planes that returned were badly shot up.

It became obvious to General Eaker and his staff that long-range daylight missions into Germany would be a real problem. Fighter escorts to provide protection against the

German fighters were not available for missions deep into Germany. The Luftwaffe inflicted heavy damage on any attacking force that was without accompanying fighter protection.

Weather was also a great problem for the inexperienced American pilots. In spite of these difficulties, Eaker began developing more plans for risky, long-range, unescorted missions deep into Germany. These would attack the Messerschmitt and Focke-Wulfe aircraft factories where the enemy planes were built.

But suddenly bombing missions from England were called off. Operation Torch, the invasion of North Africa by Allied forces, was under way. The Eighth Air Force was ordered to send over 100 planes to Africa to support that vital campaign. At the same time, orders came from the Allied high command in London to bomb the German U-boat bases on the French Atlantic coast once again.

Luftwaffe Tactics Improve

Even when Allied fighters escorted daylight bombing missions, German Me 109s and FW 190s were developing new methods of attack. The German fighters were to attack from below and behind an American bomber, where only one set of guns could return fire. Another even more daring

The Focke-Wulfe 190, armed with machine guns, cannon and rockets, destroyed hundreds of American and British bombers in combat over Germany.

USAAF B-24 Liberator bombers drop their bombs on German targets on D-Day. One plane has already gone down in smoke.

maneuver was the head-on attack. Fearless Focke-Wulfe pilots would attack head-on from the twelve o'clock position with all six machine guns blazing at the poorly defended nose of the bombers.

American bombers were blown up or severely damaged again and again. Some crew members parachuted safely to the ground to spend the rest of the war in a German prison camp. Hundreds more died with their planes.

Round-the-Clock Bombing Approved

In early January 1943, President Franklin D. Roosevelt of the United States and British Prime Minister Winston Churchill met with other Allied leaders at Casablanca in North Africa. While there, they approved the continued conquest of North Africa and the invasion of Italy. They also approved long-range bombing of military, industrial and civilian targets in Germany. The Eighth Air Force would conduct high-altitude daylight raids on specific targets. The RAF Bomber Command would conduct nighttime saturation bombing raids of major industrial cities.

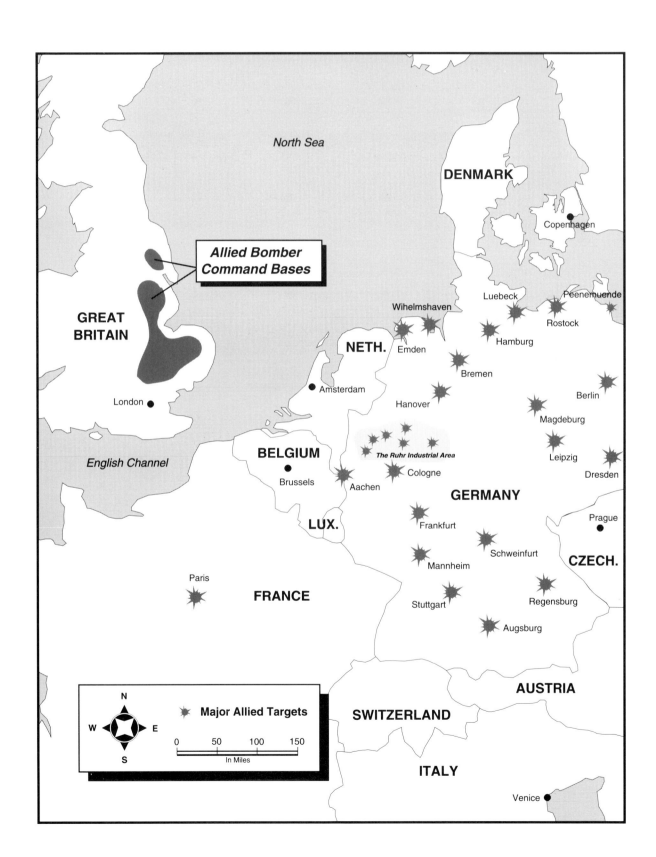

Chapter 5

BIG BOMBERS AND LITTLE FRIENDS

One thing the B-17 Flying Fortresses and the B-24 Liberators needed for their dangerous daytime raids was the protection of fighter escorts, or "little friends," as the bomber crews called the small single-seat fighter escorts. Germans attacked the bomber formations the moment they crossed the English Channel headed toward Germany. Fast, long-range and well-armed Allied fighters were needed to fight off the attacking bandits.

During the first Eighth Air Force raids flown in 1942 and 1943 there were a few RAF Spitfires and early model USAAF P-38 and P-51 fighters available for escort duty. But they had limited range, so the bombers had to fly most of the way to and from their targets without fighter protection. More and longer-range little friends were needed. The Luftwaffe attacked formations and destroyed American bombers as soon as the escorting fighters had to turn back for lack of fuel. The heavy protective armor and defensive weapons on the B-17s and B-24s, as well as their tightly knit formations, were not enough to prevent heavy losses.

Daylight Raids Continue

Learning the art of high-level precision bombing was a costly affair. First of all, the men who flew the B-17s and B-24s had little experience. Most of them were in their early twenties. They were well-trained in their jobs, but they were all inexperienced in combat.

High-level flying is technically and physically difficult. Flying at high altitudes requires the use of oxygen, and temperatures often fall far below freezing. Every bomber crew member was equipped with heavy flying clothes, a parachute, oxygen equipment, a radio headset and microphone, a flak or bullet-proof vest and a pistol and a knife.

The gunners at the middle of the craft fired their machine guns through side ports, which were open to the freezing air. The gunner in the revolving ball turret hanging beneath a B-17 was in cramped quarters for as long as ten hours at a time.

On October 13, 1943, there was a raid on Munster, Germany. Even after a year of combat experience, only one plane returned out of the 13 that had left England. The skills of flying in combat had to be learned and relearned as new crews arrived from the United States almost daily.

The average airman flew only 15 missions, although he was scheduled to return home after 25. Death, wounds, illness and fatigue shortened the tour of duty for many. Flak (antiaircraft fire), attacking fighters, mechanical failure and combat fatigue were taking a heavy toll. As more of their buddies were lost in combat, each crew member wondered if his turn would be next.

500-Plane Missions Become Routine

As the bombing of Fortress Europe became more intensified in late 1943 and 1944, missions by huge formations of heavy bombers became regular events. And the problems became even greater. Every mission took weeks of planning. Aerial photographs, mission reports and intelligence from every possible source had to be gathered and analyzed. Targets had to be chosen and air crews thoroughly briefed.

The vast number of aircraft and the bombs, ammunition and supplies they demanded had to be prepared. Ground

Inside a B-17 Flying Fortress, two waist gunners rest beside their .50 caliber machine guns while on the way to a target in Germany.

crews worked all through the night preparing their big birds for each mission. This all happened before a mission was ready to leave the ground.

A 500-plane mission utilized aircraft from as many as a dozen different groups, taking off from as many different air bases. Squadrons made up of a dozen or so aircraft had to join up with three or four other squadrons to form a group; groups had to join up with other groups to form a wing; and wings had to join together to make up the giant formation.

At takeoff time planes would line up, waiting for orders. When the order finally came, planes would take their position on the runway one after the other and take off at intervals of often less than a minute. Loaded to the limit with bombs, ammunition and fuel, each plane needed all the power it could generate and would use the full length of a runway before liftoff.

With brakes locked, the pilot would advance the throttles so that engines were roaring at full power. Releasing the brakes, the pilot would steer his craft slowly down the runway. The pilot would hold the plane on the ground until full flying speed had been reached. He would then gradually pull back on the control column to lift his ten-ton aircraft into the air. Climbing carefully, each plane circled to join up with its squadron mates.

On a large mission of 500 or more aircraft, it took up to two hours of circling and joining together before the force was complete. Midair collisions happened often. Engine failure caused planes to drop out and return to base. Bad weather often caused missions to be cancelled.

But on most missions the force would become a single mass formation and head toward its assigned target. A pathfinder aircraft with the command navigator aboard would lead this aerial armada toward Germany, 300 or more miles away. And that's when the real trouble began.

German Radar and Antiaircraft

In addition to the swarms of Luftwaffe fighters there were other dangers to be faced. Bad weather with cloudy skies was common. Extra-tight formations were called for. Soon after leaving the English coast behind, German radar would already have identified the approaching aircraft. Antiaircraft batteries firing high-explosive shells would fill the air with flak as Allied bombers came within range. Luftwaffe fighters and more flak were always waiting as radar stations along the attack route directed action against the attacking bombers.

Long-Range Fighters to the Rescue

As the air war over Europe progressed, so did the development of USAAF fighter aircraft. American factories were turning out more powerful fighters with better engines and more guns. Twin-tail, twin-engine P-38 Lightnings, sleek

"Little friends" in formation. The P-38 Lockheed Lightning (top), *the P-51 North American Mustang* (center) *and the P-47 Republic Thunderbolt were long-range fighter escorts for bombing missions over Germany.*

P-51 Mustangs and heavy P-47 Thunderbolt fighters were becoming available in huge numbers. Disposable external fuel tanks gave them the range needed to accompany the bombers far into German airspace. The fighters' main tanks still filled with fuel, the external tanks would be dropped when the fighter escorts met the attacking Luftwaffe fighters. By March 1944, P-51s were able to provide fighter escort all the way to Berlin.

After the Mission

The most dangerous part of any bombing mission came after the bombs were dropped. The badly shot-up formations had to regroup and head back toward England. They were constantly under attack in the air and from the ground. Formations became ragged and filled with holes as aircraft were blown out of the sky. Normal protective crossfire from within a tight formation was no longer possible. And there were often dead and wounded to be cared for aboard a damaged plane.

On landing, a bomber crew or fighter pilot was immediately debriefed. Intelligence officers got every bit of information about each mission from crew members while it was still fresh in their minds. Film was removed from bomb-bay and gun cameras to analyze bombing and gunnery results. Ground crews got to work repairing damaged aircraft, patching up flak and bullet holes and getting them ready for the next flight. The crews then hit the sack to rest up and get ready for the next mission — and pray they would stay alive until that wonderful 25th mission was completed.

A smiling A-20 crew head for debriefing after returning from a successful mission.

Chapter 6

THREE DISASTROUS MISSIONS

The bombing of Fortress Europe by the Eighth Air Force and RAF Bomber Command eventually ended in complete victory. It took almost five long years. On the way to victory three courageous but costly missions stood out: Ploesti, Schweinfurt and Regensburg.

These missions represent the bitter lessons learned, the many failed missions, the hundreds of aircraft destroyed and the lives lost on the road to victory. They do not take away from the hundreds of successful missions, the heroism of the air crews or the strong will of the leaders. They do point out the high cost of victory and the fact that, even in victory, the cost in lost lives and aircraft was terrible.

The Ploesti Raid

In July 1943, successful heavy raids were being conducted throughout Germany. Major cities such as Hamburg were virtually destroyed by night and day mass bombings. During the last week of July 1943, known as "blitz week," a dozen other industrial targets were bombed and damaged.

American bomber groups had suffered heavily on these raids. Over 80 aircraft were lost to German fighter attacks and flak. Air crews were exhausted from flying one mission after another. Aircraft needed repairs and more than 100 B-24 Liberators had been sent to Africa, weakening the operating strength of the Eighth Air Force.

While experiencing these heavy losses, the Allies did achieve excellent results in their bombing missions. However, something had to be done to stop the Luftwaffe fighters. One bomber mission after another returned minus a dozen or more bombers lost to the skilled pilots of the attacking Me 109s and FW 190s.

Operation Pointblank

To offset the great losses of U.S. bombers, the Allied high command decided to launch Operation Pointblank — an all-out attack against the Luftwaffe's supply sources. Aircraft factories and related industries were major targets. The first target selected was Germany's main source of aircraft fuel, the oil-refining plants near Ploesti, Romania.

A force of 200 B-24 Liberator bombers was gathered together at bases in Libya in North Africa. Weeks of intensive training followed, involving low-level attacks against simulated Ploesti targets built in the Libyan deserts. Commanded by Major General Lewis Brereton, the Ploesti raiders took off on their ill-fated mission on August 1, 1943.

Low-Level Surprise Attack Planned

The round-trip from Libya to Ploesti was 2,700 miles. Each aircraft carried a full load of fuel and bombs and extra fuel in external drop tanks. It was a long and dangerous mission under any circumstances. In addition, in order to achieve surprise, the 178 B-24 Liberators flew only a few hundred feet above the land and water en route to the target. For greater accuracy they were to bomb at rooftop level.

Bad weather and navigational errors made the long mission even more difficult. The huge attacking force became divided. As a result they did not attack all at once as planned. In addition, the defending antiaircraft batteries and Luftwaffe fighter squadrons had learned exactly when the raiders would arrive.

The Ploesti defenders were prepared for the poorly executed attack. All told, 53 B-24s were lost, 55 were severely damaged, 310 U.S. airmen were killed and over 100 were taken prisoner. Despite some heavy damage, the Ploesti refineries were back in full production within a few weeks.

Schweinfurt and Regensburg

The Messerschmitt aircraft factory in Regensburg and the ball-bearing plants in Schweinfurt were two other targets selected as part of Operation Pointblank. A successful attack on Schweinfurt would cut off the supply of ball bearings (used to reduce friction in moving parts) for planes, trucks, tanks and other military equipment. The aircraft factory at Regensburg, if destroyed, would reduce the number of Luftwaffe fighters.

A B-17 heads back to England after bombing the ball-bearing factories at Schweinfurt.

Again, as in the case of the Ploesti raid, bad luck and operational errors led to disaster. On August 17, 1943, heavy fog in England delayed the Regensburg attack. A group of some 150 B-17s led by Colonel Curtis LeMay sat and waited in the fog. In spite of the weather, however, they took off and headed for Germany. The P-47 groups that were to provide fighter protection for the bombers never got off the ground because of the weather.

The Schweinfurt mission was scheduled to take off at the same time. They were delayed more than three hours before taking off. They too were without fighter protection. What had been planned as a heavy one-two punch delivered at two targets at the same time became separate missions. Luftwaffe fighters in full strength attacked the two groups as each approached its target.

300 Bandits Attack

The German early-warning radar system spotted the huge forces of B-17s as they crossed the English Channel. LeMay's five groups were jumped by bandits immediately. The enemy used machine guns and rockets and even dropped bombs set to explode within the bomber formations. Daring head-on group attacks by the Luftwaffe downed one B-17 after another. Before the first bombs were dropped, 17 Flying Fortresses were lost.

After leaving a bombed and flaming Regensburg behind them, LeMay's groups headed south toward landing fields in Africa. After their first attack, the German fighters landed to refuel and then attacked again. Four more B-17s were lost leaving the target. It would have been even worse, but the Germans were taken by surprise when the mission headed for Africa instead of back to England.

Schweinfurt Raid Another Disaster

Because the two missions were three hours apart, the Luftwaffe was able to attack each group separately. There-

After being hit by German antiaircraft fire, a B-26 Martin Marauder, with one engine shot away, goes down in flames.

fore, each mission was attacked in full force repeatedly. Nevertheless, the Schweinfurt ball-bearing factories were bombed heavily with incendiary and high-explosive bombs. But 36 U.S. bombers and more than 300 men were lost during the raid. Fortunately American P-47 fighters joined the battered B-17s on their return flight to fight off the bandits during the last portion of the return trip to England.

As was the case at Ploesti, the damage done in these two costly raids was limited. In spite of the loss of more than 60 American bombers and hundreds of brave airmen, the German factories were still able to function.

Following these costly raids, long-range missions without fighter escort were called off. They were not resumed until the new long-range P-51s and P-47s arrived a few months later to provide the needed protection.

Chapter 7

D-DAY
FROM THE AIR

Operation Overlord, the invasion of Europe by Allied forces, began on D-Day, June 6, 1944. This was a heroic effort by hundreds of thousands of Allied troops who landed on the beaches and fields of Normandy in France.

All branches of the USAAF and RAF played a large part in the success of the D-Day landings. Key German defense positions were hit before, during and following the D-Day invasion. Air cover and support for the troops landing on the beaches and as they headed inland were provided at all times.

Long-range, high-level bombing attacks on the enemy's industrial cities continued. Special targets that needed to be destroyed to make way for the D-Day landings were hit. Thousands of fighter-bombers and light bombers made low-level attacks on German defenses during the D-Day landings and in the weeks that followed.

The Transportation Plan

British Field Marshal Bernard Montgomery, commander of Overlord ground forces, wanted the railroads and rail yards that supported German coastal defenses demolished. This would halt, or at least slow down, the movement of reinforcements and supplies to the German coastal defenders as Operation Overlord began.

Some 75 specific rail yards containing hundreds of locomotives, thousands of freight cars, troop trains and repair shops were targeted. The RAF and the Eighth Air Force

USAAF heavy bombers successfully bombed Nazi industrial targets throughout France and Germany.

shared these targets. All of them were hit again and again. RAF Bomber Command alone flew over 10,000 missions against railroad targets with great success.

Mass Bombing One Key to Success

On D-Day the RAF flew 1,136 heavy bomber missions. The USAAF flew an equal number as wave after wave of B-17s and B-24s bombed German shore installations along the French coast. Their targets were German coastal guns, beach defenses, radar sites and airfields.

Low-level fighter-bombers also attacked in great numbers. Allied forces fighting in France needed all the direct air support they could get. P-38s, P-47s and P-51s were provided with greater firepower and carried bombs and rockets. The A-20 Havoc and B-26 Marauder light bombers were equipped with additional forward-firing machine guns plus rockets and their normal bombloads.

Troop Carriers, Paratroopers and Gliders

On the night before D-Day a new type of aerial warfare was added. The Ninth Troop Carrier Command sent a force of over 800 C-47 transports carrying paratroopers to be dropped behind enemy lines in France. Another 100 transports towed gliders loaded with men and equipment to join up with the paratroopers. Towed to their landing areas, the gliders cut loose from their towplanes. The glider pilots steered the powerless aircraft to a landing on the farmlands of Normandy.

Taking off in darkness and delivering their cargoes of paratroopers and gliders before dawn was a superhuman task. Although a good number of this force were shot down or lost their way, most of these airborne troops landed as planned.

Air-Ground Support Missions

Tactical air power, as aerial ground-support is called, was put into use at once in France. This type of air war took various forms. One tactic was to destroy enemy aircraft and airfields within striking distance of the invading Allied armies. Aircraft of all types attacked these targets.

Another tactic of a ground-support air force was to disrupt enemy transport and communications. The supply lines of counterattacking German panzer and infantry units were strafed and bombed continually. Daring low-level attacks were aimed at enemy railroads, highways, supply trucks, troop carriers and trains as they headed toward the Normandy battlefields.

A third tactic was to attack enemy troops, tanks, artillery and ground defenses that were blocking the advancing Allied troops. Strikes against specific enemy targets, often within a few hundred yards of Allied attackers, were made on demand. Trained air controllers with the ground troops radioed for help as needed.

The courageous fighter-bomber pilots flew as many as

B-25 Mitchell medium bombers armed with 75mm cannon and .50 caliber machine guns in the nose provided close-in air support for Allied forces.

three and four missions a day. Airfields in France were built quickly so that the attacking Allied planes could be as close to the front lines as possible to provide immediate attacks on enemy strongpoints.

Luftwaffe Airfields and Aircraft Attacked

As the USAAF and the RAF grew in strength, the Luftwaffe shrank. Not only were German aircraft factories being damaged, but more and more Luftwaffe aircraft were being destroyed in the air and on the ground. Airfields in France, Holland, Belgium and Germany became regular targets. If bomber formations were not attacked by bandits, the bombers' escort fighters would swoop down to ground level to attack enemy airfields and aircraft on the ground. And of course the low-flying Allied fighter-bombers would attack any enemy airfields and aircraft. With complete air support and increasing air superiority, Operation Overlord moved ahead on schedule.

Chapter 8

THE FINAL CONFLICT

For more than four years the USAAF and the RAF worked together to destroy the Luftwaffe and the factories that supported the German war effort. Not only did they possess aircraft of high quality in large numbers but they also possessed superior manpower. Not that the Luftwaffe aircraft or pilots were inferior in any way. The Me 109s and FW 190s were the equal of any American or RAF fighter aircraft up through 1944. Luftwaffe pilots were experienced and skillful.

Following D-Day in mid-1944, rapid improvements were made to each succeeding model of USAAF and RAF aircraft. With German factories being destroyed by Allied bombing, the Luftwaffe could not make such improvements or even replace aircraft lost in combat.

Thousands of new pilots joined the Allied forces each year. The Germans were unable to even replace the skilled and experienced pilots they had lost, let alone add to their dwindling air force.

Germany Fights on with Jets and Rockets

Germany had tremendous technical skills that, if properly used, could have changed the outcome of the war. As early as 1942 the Me 262A, a jet-propelled fighter, was ready for production. It flew 150 miles an hour faster than Allied fighters. For some reason Hitler delayed the production of this great jet fighter. Finally, in 1944, the Me 262 went into production and over 1,000 were produced. However, Germany no longer had the pilots to fly them, nor

The Me 262 was the first operational German jet fighter. It did not see action until too late in the war to do the Germans any good.

enough fuel to keep them in the air to combat the numerically superior Allied air forces.

Other weapons that showed German genius at work were the V-1 and V-2 rockets. The V stands for *Vergeltung-swaffen* (German for "revenge weapon"). The V-1, or buzz-bomb or doodlebug, was a 26-foot-long pilotless jet-propelled aircraft that carried a bombload of 1,870 pounds. It was used during 1944 from bases in France or Belgium. Upon reaching its target (usually London) pre-set controls stopped its engine, and the flying bomb would crash to the ground with great damage to property and many civilian casualties. Following D-Day, Allied troops destroyed these sites and removed the V-1 from action.

The V-2 was a long-range full-scale rocket that was developed and manufactured at a base at Peenemunde Island in northeastern Germany. The V-2 was a fully rocket-propelled missile that carried a load of high explosives 200 miles. Because it was blasted to great heights and plunged straight down on its target, it was undetected until shortly before striking the ground.

The V-2 finally came into frequent use in 1945. Over 1,200 of these giant rockets landed on targets in Great Britain, causing over 10,000 casualties, extensive property damage and a demoralizing effect on British citizens. Fortunately the war ended before greater use could be made of this deadly weapon.

Chapter 9

VICTORY OVER FORTRESS EUROPE

In the final months of the war, Allied air activity continued to increase on all fronts. The Fifteenth Air Force joined the bombing of Fortress Europe following the surrender of Italy. Under the command of Major General Nathan Twining, American bombers struck at German factories and bases in Austria, Hungary and Romania.

Oil and synthetic fuel production facilities were the main Allied targets. On November 2, 1944, 1,000 bombers plus 900 fighters targeted a synthetic oil plant at Merseberg, Germany. Since this was considered an important production plant by the Germans, every German fighter aircraft available within flying distance was called into action. The Luftwaffe lost 208 planes that day and still failed to prevent the successful bombing of the refinery.

Carpet Tactical Bombing

In late 1944 and on into 1945 the rapidly advancing British and American ground forces called on air force help continuously. In one mission, called Operation Cobra, General Jimmy Doolittle, now in command of the Eighth Air Force, responded to a request for help in opening a hole only nine miles long and a few miles wide in the German lines. Attacking aircraft dropped over 3,000 tons of explosives within that narrow strip of land. The German defense was shattered, and American forces streamed through the hole to advance deeper into Germany.

With little interference from the Luftwaffe, similar close-

German dictator Adolf Hitler and his staff wade through the ruins of a bombed German city as World War II draws to a close.

support strafing and bombing took place every day. From flights of as few as four or five P-47s to full-sized squadrons and groups, the Allied air forces were at work daily. They helped open the way for the tanks and infantry surging forward into Germany toward its capital city, Berlin.

Berlin in Ruins

Along with many other major German cities, Berlin was almost completely destroyed by Allied bombs. Hitler went into hiding and most of Nazi Germany was without leaders. With no air force and with the ground army having little fuel and ammunition, the war was almost over. The skies belonged to the Allies.

Hermann Goering, chief of the Luftwaffe, said before he committed suicide, "Without the United States Air Force the war would still be going on . . . and it would not be going on on German soil."

The Allied Bombers Get Through

As the air battles over Fortress Europe drew to a close, Italian General Douhet's theories proved to be correct. The Allied bombers did get through to their targets. The superior bombing forces of the USAAF and the RAF destroyed the enemy's bombers and fighters in the air and on the ground. They destroyed the factories where enemy aircraft were being built. The successful air battles opened and paved the way for the victorious Allied ground troops that obtained the final surrender of the German nation and its military forces.

The Luftwaffe, once in command of the skies over Europe, had become the defeated enemy. Previously filling the air in giant swarms, by 1945 fewer and fewer bandits took to the air to fight the giant Allied raids that continued day and night. The Luftwaffe was slowly dying as the Allies' high-flying bombers continued to destroy German aircraft factories and airfields.

A proud bombardment squadron saluted all of the Allied nations with a display of bombs that were soon to be dropped on German targets.

Flying high above advancing Allied ground forces, a huge formation of B-17 Flying Fortresses forms condensation trails as they head toward Germany and final victory.

High level or low level, the USAAF and the RAF were free to attack targets throughout Germany at will. The once giant Luftwaffe, designed for offensive action, was reduced to a small defensive role against a vastly superior enemy.

Air power alone did not win the war in Europe. It did its job well but at tremendous cost. Over 25,000 Allied planes were lost in combat. Some 160,000 British and American airmen died, in addition to an unknown number of German air crews. The bombing done by the mighty Allied aerial armadas struck military and civilian targets alike. Over 300,000 German civilians died.

Hitler's Fortress Europe had been bombed to final defeat. The bombers did get through and help end the war.

GLOSSARY

air raid An attack by enemy aircraft.

Allies The nations that joined together during World War II to defeat Germany, Japan and Italy: France, Great Britain, the Soviet Union and the United States.

antiaircraft Large cannon or machine guns used to shoot at attacking aircraft.

armament Any military weapons.

blitzkrieg Means "lightning war" in German.

flak Exploding antiaircraft shells.

incendiary bomb A bomb containing materials that will start a fire.

jet-propelled Powered by jet engines that derive their power from the ejection of burning gases.

Luftwaffe The German air force before and during World War II.

mission A combat operation assigned to an individual or unit.

navigator A crew member who plots the course of a ship or an aircraft.

Nazi A member of the National Socialist party that ruled Germany from 1933 to 1945 under Adolf Hitler.

panzer A German tank.

paratroopers Soldiers trained to jump from aircraft using parachutes.

pathfinder aircraft An aircraft that guides a bomber formation to an enemy target.

radar Radio equipment that detects airplanes and ships and determines their distance, speed and altitude. Short for <u>RA</u>dio <u>D</u>etection <u>A</u>nd <u>R</u>anging.

rocket An explosive weapon propelled by hot gases ejected from the rear.

saturation bombing Blanketing a target area with a large quantity of bombs dropped by a number of aircraft.

sortie One mission by a single aircraft against an enemy.

strafe To attack ground targets with machine guns from an aircraft.

synthetic fuel Alternative liquid or gaseous fuel that can be used instead of gasoline in motor vehicles or aircraft.

U-boat German submarine; short for *Unterseeboot*, or undersea boat.

Zeppelin A rigid airship with a long cigar-shaped body supported by internal gas cells filled with a lighter-than-air gas.

INDEX